GROW IT AGAIN

written by
Elizabeth MacLeod

illustrated by

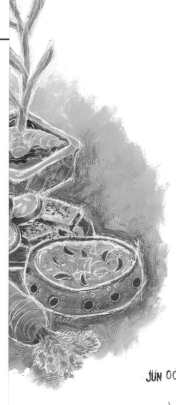

In memory of Alison, with much love

Published in Canada by
Kids Can Press Ltd.
29 Birch Avenue
Toronto, ON M4V 1E2

Published in the U.S. by
Kids Can Press Ltd.
85 River Rock Drive, Suite 202
Buffalo, NY 14207

Edited by Laura Ellis
Designed by Julia Naimska
Printed in Hong Kong by Wing King Tong Co. Ltd.

CM 99 0 9 8 7 6 5 4 3 2 1

Canadian Cataloguing in Publication Data
MacLeod, Elizabeth
Grow it again

(Kids can do it)
ISBN 1-55074-558-1

1. Gardening — Juvenile literature.   I. Price, Caroline.   II. Title.   III. Series.

SB457.M32 1999   j635   C98-932224-6

Contents

Introduction

*You may find it hard to believe,
but the makings of a fantastic garden
are probably in your kitchen right now.
Next time you're helping your dad or
mom prepare dinner, don't put those
carrot tops in the compost or throw out
the seeds in that apple core — instead,
try growing them. Turn a peanut into
an unusual flower or a beet top
into a leafy plant.*

*Some of the plants you grow
will flower and even give you fruit, and
all of them will give you great-looking
leaves. It's an inexpensive and fun way to
grow plants for decorating your room or
giving as gifts. Some of the plants grow
from root tops, others from seeds, bulbs or
tubers. And be sure to check out the
recipes, ideas for decorating pots, and
other activities that are scattered
throughout the book.*

MATERIALS

PUT IT IN A POT

You can grow your plants in clay or plastic flowerpots, as well as many other containers — see pages 15 and 40 for ideas. Whatever container you use, wash it well with soap and hot water, scrub off any dirt, rinse away all the soap, and be sure it is completely dry before you begin planting.

THE DIRT ON SOIL

Plant your seeds and roots in fresh potting soil instead of bringing soil in from outside. Your garden soil may have insects in it or carry plant diseases that will love the warmth of your home.

LIGHTEN UP

The best place to grow most plants is in a sunny window, since plants like at least eight hours of sun each day. Indoor plants get much less light than plants grown outside so unless you live somewhere that receives a lot of sunlight, there's little risk that your plants will get too much sun. But if your plants look droopy and you know you're giving them enough water, try moving them a little farther from the window.

Plants need light and will grow toward it to get as much as they can. Turn your plants regularly so they grow straight and don't lean to one side.

WATER POWER

Check your plants daily to make sure they have enough water, especially in spring and summer when sunlight is strong and your plants are growing quickly. When you're watering plants in a pot, feel the soil. If it is dry to the touch, it's time to water the plant. Add enough water so that it just begins to run out the drainage hole in the bottom of the pot, then pour away the extra water.

ROCK ON

Most plants will be happiest if you put a layer of stones in the bottom of their pots, below the soil. That lets any extra water drain out so that the roots don't sit in it.

Make sure the stones that you use are clean and free of disease. Use new stones that you've rinsed in hot water and let dry, or wash old stones in hot, soapy water, rinse them to remove all soap, and let them dry.

T I P S

HOT, HOT, HOT

Many of the plants in this book are more at home in the tropics, so if you're keeping your plants on a windowsill, be sure it's not too cold for them. Most plants also prefer to be far from drafts, so choose a sunny place where your plants will be warm and undisturbed, and they'll grow best.

MINI-GREENHOUSE

Some plants like warm, moist air, especially when they're first sprouting. An easy way to provide the right air for a plant is to cover the pot with a clear plastic bag or a piece of plastic wrap. Keep checking your plant and water it when the soil seems a little dry. When you see shoots coming up, it's time to remove the bag.

GROW BETTER

Feeding your plants with fertilizer will help them to produce beautiful leaves. If you grow your plants in fresh potting soil, they won't need fertilizer for about two months. After that, fertilize your plants (follow the directions on the fertilizer package) when you see new leaves and shoots. For plant tops or bulbs growing on stones, add a pinch or drop of fertilizer to the water about once a month. Be careful — if you overfertilize your plants, you may burn their roots.

PESKY PESTS

If you see bugs or webs on one of your plants, quickly move it away from your other plants to keep the rest of your garden from becoming infected. Pick off any bugs that you can see. You can also wash the leaves with soapy water, but be sure to rinse them in clear water afterward.

Spraying or washing your plants twice a week with clear, lukewarm water will help keep pests away. Don't use an insect spray on any plants that you will eat.

BETTER THE ODDS

Some seeds and roots won't grow no matter how well you treat them. So you're not disappointed, plant a few at a time. If they all grow, move the extras into another pot or have a lush garden all in one pot.

MOVE IT

Many of the plants you grow have fragile root systems and don't like to be transplanted. They're easier to move if you wait until they have strong stems and a few leaves. When a plant has grown too large for its pot and needs a larger one, move as much of the soil around its roots as you can.

7

TAKE IT FROM THE TOP

Many plant and root tops will sprout leaves and grow into a beautiful garden. And most just need water, sun and stones — no soil — to get started.

Start your top-down garden with the plants described in this section, then try any others that you like, such as parsnips. Produce from health food stores often grows best because it usually hasn't been treated to keep it from sprouting. If you grow plant tops that already show buds or tiny leaves, you'll have a garden sooner.

WATER ALERT

Check your plant top daily to make sure that the cut side is always in water. If the water gets cloudy, pour it away and replace it.

FAST GROWERS

Plant tops will give you leaves faster than almost any plants you can grow. You'll see them in just a few days. The downside is that some may not last long — after a few weeks they might start to droop. Replace them with new plant tops and you'll soon have another great-looking garden.

CLEAN UP YOUR ACT

Make sure the stones that you use are clean and free of disease. Use new stones that you've rinsed in hot water and let dry, or wash old stones in hot, soapy water, rinse them well to remove all soap, and let them dry. Don't worry if your stones become covered with algae and turn green — your root tops will still grow well.

Carrot

Keep a garden of carrots always on the grow by adding more carrot tops every time you eat carrots.

GROW IT RIGHT

1 Place a layer of stones in a bowl or dish with sides.

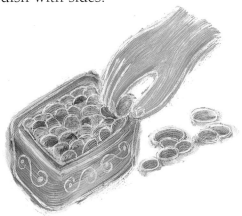

2 Depending on the size of the carrot, ask an adult to cut a piece off the top that's between 0.5 cm (¼ in.) thick (for a small carrot) and 1 cm (½ in.) thick (for a large one). You'll probably find that bigger carrots grow better.

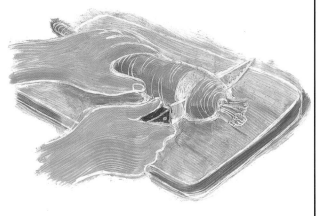

3 Place the carrot top, cut side down, on the stones. Keep your carrot top in a sunny window and check every day to make sure the cut side is in water.

KEEP IT GREEN

• Carrot tops look even better if you grow a few of them together in a shallow bowl or dish.

OTHER IDEAS

You can grow beets in the same way. When you cut the top off the beet, leave 1 cm (½ in.) of beet attached to the top. When the leaves die off, keep watering your beet top and in a few months it may flower.

Carrot-pineapple muffins

After you've prepared these great-tasting muffins, try growing the carrot tops.

YOU WILL NEED

375 mL	all-purpose flour	1½ c.
250 mL	white sugar	1 c.
5 mL	baking powder	1 tsp.
5 mL	baking soda	1 tsp.
5 mL	cinnamon	1 tsp.
1 mL	salt	¼ tsp.
150 mL	vegetable oil	⅔ c.
2	eggs, beaten	
5 mL	vanilla	1 tsp.
250 mL	carrots, finely grated	1 c.
284-mL can	crushed pineapple, drained well	10-oz. can

UTENSILS
muffin pans for 18 muffins, sifter, measuring cups, measuring spoons, large bowl, wooden spoon

1 Preheat the oven to 180°C (350°F) and lightly grease the muffin cups.

2 Sift the flour, sugar, baking powder, baking soda, cinnamon and salt into a large bowl. Add the remaining ingredients and mix until well combined.

3 Fill each of the prepared muffin cups about two-thirds full of batter. Ask an adult to help you bake the muffins for 20 minutes or until golden brown. Makes 18 muffins.

HOE, HOE, HOE

What's orange and blasts out of the ground?

A jet-propelled carrot!

Yam

Whether you call them yams or sweet potatoes, you'll find that long, thin yams are best for growing. Look for one with roots or small buds.

GROW IT RIGHT

1 Place a layer of stones in a bowl or dish with sides. Use a deep bowl or container since this top grows lots of roots.

2 You'll need a piece of yam that's about 5 cm (2 in.) long. Ask an adult to cut it off the top of the yam — that's the rounder, less pointy end.

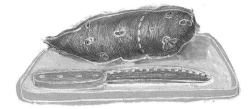

3 Place the yam piece, top side up, on the stones. Keep your yam in a sunny window.

KEEP IT GREEN

• Check daily to make sure the cut side of your yam is always under water.

• When the leaves on your yam first begin to grow, they'll be purple and will slowly turn green.

• If your yam hasn't sprouted leaves in a week, start again with one from a health food store.

CAN YOU BELIEVE IT?

In the South Pacific, yams can weigh as much as 45 kg (100 lb.). That's about the average weight of a 13-year-old kid.

Pineapple

A pineapple plant has lots of long spiky leaves and will grow for years.

GROW IT RIGHT

1 Place a layer of stones in a bowl or dish with sides.

2 Ask an adult to cut off the top of the pineapple just below the leaves, leaving about 2 cm (¾ in.) of fruit attached.

3 Grow your pineapple on stones for about two to three weeks until roots appear. Then move it into a pot filled with soil — if you can, add some sand to make the kind of soil pineapples like best. Be sure to cover the base of the pineapple top with soil.

KEEP IT GREEN

• If you don't use your pineapple right away, spray the leaves with water to keep them green, healthy and fresh until you can grow them.

CAN YOU BELIEVE IT?

The pineapple is a symbol of welcome. Native people of the Caribbean islands used to put pineapples at the entrances to their villages to let visitors know that they were welcome.

Painting pots

If you're giving friends some of your plants as gifts, why not give them in decorated pots? You can paint plastic or clay pots, or glass dishes. Make sure the pots are clean and dry before you decorate them. Clay pots are porous, so water will seep from the inside to the outside and blister any paint you've brushed on. To prevent this, add two coats of acrylic varnish to the outside of the pot and let dry before you decorate.

Try these painting ideas to decorate your pots:

• Squeeze on designs using tubes of fabric paint.

• Paint on a pattern with a brush and stencil or a sponge. Use acrylic paint. You can also add a design using stamps, either ones you buy or ones you make yourself by cutting a pattern into a pencil eraser or potato.

• Brush on a solid color of paint. When it is completely dry, add a design with another color of paint. Or glue on beads, shells, buttons, etc.

• Splatter on paint using a toothbrush and a Popsicle stick or old pencil. Dip the brush bristles in paint, aim them toward the pot and brush the stick or pencil across the bristles. When that paint is dry, wash the toothbrush thoroughly, then try splattering on different colors.

• Dribble on paint by dipping a stick in paint and letting it drip onto the pot.

Turnip

Not one of your favorite vegetables to eat? You may change your mind when you see the great garden it grows.

GROW IT RIGHT

1 Place a layer of stones in a bowl or dish with sides.

2 Ask an adult to cut a piece off the top of the turnip (the end with a few leaf buds and no point or root hairs) that's between 1 cm (½ in.) thick (for a small turnip) and 2.5 cm (1 in.) thick (for a large one).

3 Place the turnip top, cut side down, on the stones. Keep your turnip top in a sunny window.

KEEP IT GREEN

• Give your turnip top lots of water and sun and it may grow small yellow flowers.

• If your turnip hasn't sprouted leaves in a week, start again with one from a health food store.

HOE, HOE, HOE

What do you do if you find a blue turnip?

Try to cheer it up!

OTHER IDEAS

Plant radishes in the same way. Use big, fresh, solid ones and cut a piece off the top that's at least 0.5 cm (¼ in.) thick.

Carton garden

Milk and juice cartons make inexpensive but terrific planters. Thoroughly wash the carton with soap and water. When it's dry, glue the open end closed. Cut out one side, as shown. Paint the outside with thick poster paint or latex paint. Place a layer of stones on the bottom of the carton, then add your plants.

GIVE A GARDEN

A group of plants makes a beautiful gift for a friend or relative. For instance, arrange a few different plant tops in a decorated container (see pages 13, 40 and this page) — place the tops on colored stones if you like. Or, in a pot or planter, grow a group of herbs or other plants that your friend can eat and use (see pages 17, 20, 23, etc.).

Be sure to include a name tag for each plant, as well as directions on how to care for the plants. To make the name tags, use the stick-shaped tags that come with plants you buy in nurseries. Paint both sides with acrylic paint. When the paint is dry, paint on the name of the plant and, if you like, a picture of it. Prepare a care tag in the shape of a leaf and tie it to the pot.

SEED TIME

Seeds can be as small as the tiny black dots you find in kiwis or as large as the pits in avocados. They have one thing in common: if you look after them carefully, many will grow into plants for you.

HOW MANY?

The number of seeds you plant in each pot depends on the size of your seeds and your pot. In a pot 10 cm (4 in.) across, you can probably fit about five seeds. After the seeds start growing, pull out the weaker plants to give the strong ones more room.

CHILL OUT

Some seeds need to be tricked into thinking they've gone through winter before they'll sprout. To do this, place a few seeds in a small bag of moist soil, seal the bag, and place it in your refrigerator. Check the bag often to make sure the soil stays moist. You'll have to let the seeds "winterize" — scientists call it stratifying — for about six to eight weeks.

Seeds that need to be stratified include almonds, apples, chestnuts, grapes, kiwis, nectarines, peaches, pears and plums.

Bean

String beans, lima beans, black beans, pinto beans — try growing them all.

GROW IT RIGHT

1 If you're planting dried beans, rinse them, then soak them in water overnight to soften them. If you're planting fresh beans, remove the seeds from the "pods" before you plant them.

2 Place a layer of stones in the bottom of a pot and mostly fill the pot with potting soil. Gently pack down the soil to remove any air pockets.

3 Place a few beans in the pot and cover them with 1 cm (½ in.) of soil. Keep the soil moist until the seeds sprout — it'll take just a few days.

KEEP IT GREEN

• Keep your bean plants in a sunny window and water them well. In a few months they may produce small, pale pink flowers and beans that you can eat.

• If the weather outside is warm, you can try moving your bean plants to the garden. They'll grow faster and bigger outside than they will inside. Leave lots of soil around the roots when you move the plants out of their pot. Plant them in a sunny place with good soil.

HOE, HOE, HOE

What's yellow and very dangerous?

Shark-infested yellow beans!

Watermelon

Mmmm — enjoy a juicy slice of watermelon on a summer day. And don't forget to plant those seeds.

GROW IT RIGHT

1 Use seeds from a ripe watermelon. Rinse them before you plant them or the fruit around the seeds may become moldy.

2 Place a layer of stones in the bottom of a pot and mostly fill the pot with potting soil. Gently pack down the soil to remove any air pockets.

3 Place a few seeds in the pot and cover them with 1 cm (½ in.) of soil. Keep the seeds moist — you may have to water them every day.

KEEP IT GREEN

• Grow your watermelon plant in a sunny window if you want it to flower.

• Give your watermelon plant liquid fertilizer once a week.

• See page 17 for how to move your watermelon plant outside.

CAN YOU BELIEVE IT?

The biggest watermelon ever weighed 119 kg (262 lb.). That's more than most grown men weigh.

Seed necklace

Why not string seeds to make a one-of-a-kind necklace? Be sure to use seeds that you've washed carefully to remove any fruit attached to them.

• Cut a piece of thread that's as long as you'd like your necklace to be plus at least 15 cm (6 in.). Thread your needle and tie a triple knot at the other end of the thread. String on seeds by sticking the needle through them.

When the necklace is as long as you'd like, knot the ends of the thread together and cut them off. If you like, brush a little nail polish onto the knots to make them more secure.

• You can color seeds, too. Pale seeds, such as melon, orange, pea or bean, work best for this. Place the seeds in a glass or metal bowl (or other bowl that won't absorb dye) and add enough food coloring to completely cover the seeds. Let them soak for a few hours or overnight.

• Wash the seeds completely by placing them in a sieve and running water over them until no more color washes off. Place them on a glass plate and pat them dry with paper towels. Dye your seeds a variety of colors so you have lots to use.

• You can also thread seeds onto elastic cord or knot a clasp onto the ends. Experiment with stringing the seeds by poking the needle through the middle of each seed or through one end, or alternate to create a pattern. Try making bracelets, earrings, pins and other jewelry to wear with your necklace.

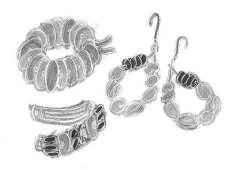

Sesame seed

You'll find this seed in the spice cupboard. The plant has really interesting leaves — they're hairy and sticky.

GROW IT RIGHT

1 Place a layer of stones in the bottom of a pot and mostly fill the pot with potting soil. Gently pack down the soil to remove any air pockets. Plant lots of sesame seeds and barely cover them with soil.

2 Cover the pot with a clear plastic bag or a piece of plastic wrap. Remove the bag in a few days when you see sprouts.

3 Keep the soil moist and place the pot in a sunny window.

KEEP IT GREEN

• If you grow all your seeds in the same pot, they may die in a few months. When you move a plant to a new pot, leave lots of soil around its roots.

• Your plant will grow pale pink flowers if you give it lots of sun. In a few months you may even get seed pods full of more sesame seeds.

OTHER IDEAS

Grow the celery seeds and mustard seeds in your spice cupboard the same way you grow sesame seeds. When the mustard sprouts are 7.5 cm (3 in.) tall, sprinkle them on salads. Try dill seeds, too. Cover the seeds with about 1 cm (½ in.) of soil and in a month you'll have leaves to use for cooking.

Sesame seed bars

A sweet, chewy snack.

YOU WILL NEED

375 mL	quick oats	1½ c.
125 mL	brown sugar	½ c.
175 mL	desiccated coconut	¾ c.
125 mL	sesame seeds	½ c.
15 mL	all-purpose flour	1 tbsp.
125 mL	cooking oil	½ c.
75 mL	liquid honey	⅓ c.
10 mL	vanilla	2 tsp.

UTENSILS
measuring cups, measuring spoons,
wooden spoon, large bowl,
3 L (9 in. x 13 in.) pan lined with
aluminum foil, spatula, kitchen knife,
waxed paper

1 Preheat the oven to 120°C (250°F).

2 Place all the ingredients in the bowl and mix thoroughly.

3 Place the mixture in the pan and pat it down with the wet spatula.

4 Ask an adult to help you bake the bars for 60 minutes on the upper rack in the oven.

5 Cool for 5 minutes. Ask an adult to cut the bars and remove them from the pan while warm. Store the bars between sheets of waxed paper.

CAN YOU BELIEVE IT?

Ever wondered where Ali Baba's secret password, "Open Sesame!" comes from? Sesame seed pods burst open when they're ripe, like a door opening when the correct magic phrase is said.

Orange

Follow these directions to grow lemon, grapefruit and tangerine seeds. All citrus trees have beautiful dark, shiny leaves.

GROW IT RIGHT

1 Place a layer of stones in the bottom of a pot and mostly fill the pot with potting soil.

2 Crush half an eggshell into tiny pieces and add it to the soil — orange trees like the nutrients in eggshells. Gently pack down the soil to remove any air pockets.

3 Use seeds from a ripe orange. Place a few seeds in the pot and barely cover them with soil.

4 Cover the pot with a clear plastic bag or a piece of plastic wrap. Keep the soil moist and place the pot in a sunny window. Remove the bag in about three weeks when you see sprouts.

KEEP IT GREEN

• Keep orange trees in a sunny spot.

• Your trees will grow slowly, but if you fertilize them they'll grow faster.

• With lots of sun and time your orange trees may flower. However, they probably won't grow fruit since they need a few trees to pollinate each other for that to happen.

HOE, HOE, HOE

What's orange and goes "slam, slam, slam, slam"?

A four-door orange!

Pea

It's difficult to get peas that are fresher than these!

GROW IT RIGHT

1 Open pea pods and use the fresh peas that are inside. Or use dried peas that you've soaked overnight.

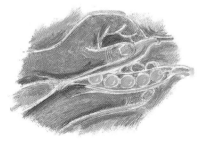

2 Place a layer of stones in the bottom of a pot and mostly fill the pot with potting soil. Gently pack down the soil to remove any air pockets. Place a few peas in the pot and cover them with about 2.5 cm (1 in.) of soil.

3 Let the soil dry out just a little each time before you water your plants.

KEEP IT GREEN

• Pea plants are vines, so you'll need to support them with sticks or pencils as they grow. Watch how the tendrils attach themselves to the supports.

• Grow your peas in a cool, sunny spot and they may flower. They may grow pea pods too, especially if you fertilize them every two weeks.

• See page 17 for how to move your pea plants outside.

CAN YOU BELIEVE IT?

During the 1600s, people in Europe were crazy about fresh peas. At one point French princes and princesses talked about almost nothing else!

Peanut

Watch the peanut flowers lose their petals, then bend and grow into the ground to form peanuts.

GROW IT RIGHT

1 Be sure to use fresh, unroasted peanuts. You can buy them in seed stores or some health food stores. Remove the shells if there are any.

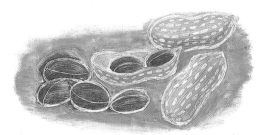

2 Place a layer of stones in the bottom of a pot and mostly fill the pot with potting soil. Gently pack down the soil to remove any air pockets.

3 Place a few peanuts in the pot and cover them with about 2.5 cm (1 in.) of soil. Keep the soil moist and place the pot in a sunny window.

KEEP IT GREEN

• Watch peanut leaves fold up at night — that's their "sleeping" position.

• To watch the flower become a peanut, plant your seeds in a clear pot and close to the edges of the pot.

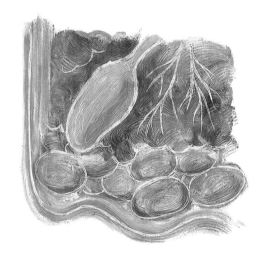

CAN YOU BELIEVE IT?

Cheese, ink and soap can all be made from peanuts. So can over 300 other products, including wood stain and insulating board. And peanuts aren't nuts at all — they belong to the same plant family as beans.

Seed painting

Peanuts are great seeds for planting, but you can also create pictures and decorate with them. Combine them with other seeds, such as melon, bean, apple, papaya or orange seeds, and you'll have lots of different shapes and sizes of seeds for your crafts.

• You can use the seeds as they are or color them — see page 19 for instructions. Be sure to dye your seeds in bowls that won't absorb the dye (such as glass or metal bowls) and choose colors that you like together.

• Use white glue to draw a design on a piece of paper and then place seeds along the design, or coat the whole surface with a thin layer of glue and cover it with seeds. Don't use too much glue or your project will take a long time to dry and, if you're working on thin paper, it may make the paper ripple. If you're covering a large area with seeds, apply glue and then seeds in small sections so the glue doesn't dry out.

• Besides using your seeds to create pictures, you can use them to cover cans to hold your pencils or other things on your desk. You may find this easier if you first cut a piece of construction paper big enough to wrap around the can and glue your seeds to the paper in a pattern you like.

When the glue is dry, glue the paper to the can. You can also use seeds to decorate a basket, special box or picture frame. If you like, glue on the larger seeds, then sprinkle on the smaller ones to fill in any gaps.

Apple

*This tree is a slow-grower,
but it will live for a long time if you
look after it carefully.*

GROW IT RIGHT

1 See page 16 for how to chill seeds before planting them. Keep your apple seeds in the fridge for about eight weeks and keep the soil moist — check it at least once a week.

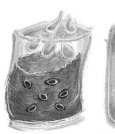

2 Place a layer of stones in the bottom of a pot and mostly fill the pot with potting soil. Gently pack down the soil to remove any air pockets. Place a few seeds in the pot and barely cover them with soil.

KEEP IT GREEN

• Apple trees naturally take a rest during the winter, so for those months keep your plants in a cool place. You'll only need to water them about twice every month. During the rest of the year you'll need to water them at least once a week.

HOE, HOE, HOE

What's worse than finding a worm in the apple you're eating?

Finding half a worm!

26

Baked apples

Especially delicious with yogurt, ice cream or whipped cream. When you core the apples, be sure to plant the seeds.

YOU WILL NEED

250 mL	water	1 c.
75 mL	white sugar	⅓ c.
75 mL	brown sugar	⅓ c.
15 mL	butter	1 tbsp.
15 mL	lemon juice	1 tbsp.
2 mL	cinnamon	½ tsp.
1 mL	nutmeg	¼ tsp.
1 mL	cloves	¼ tsp.
3	apples	
150 mL	raisins	⅔ c.

UTENSILS
measuring cups, measuring spoons, small saucepan, wooden spoon, small, sharp knife, small, shallow baking dish, large spoon

1 Preheat the oven to 190°C (375°F).

2 In the saucepan, mix the water, sugars, butter, lemon juice and spices.

3 Ask an adult to help you bring the mixture to a boil, then reduce the heat to medium so that the mixture cooks, but doesn't bubble, for 10 minutes.

4 Cut the apples in half and remove their cores. Arrange the pieces, cut side up, in the baking dish and fill them with raisins. Pour the sugar mixture over the apples.

5 Ask an adult to help you bake the apples uncovered for 30 to 45 minutes or until the apples are tender. Baste the apples often with the sugar mixture. Makes 6 servings.

Kiwi

A single kiwi fruit will provide you with hundreds of little black seeds.

GROW IT RIGHT

1 Remove all the pulp from the seeds or they may become moldy when you plant them. Use your fingers and paper towels to clean them off.

2 See page 16 for how to chill seeds. Keep your kiwi seeds in the fridge for about six weeks and keep the soil moist — check it at least once a week.

3 Place a layer of stones in the bottom of a pot and mostly fill the pot with potting soil. Gently pack down the soil to remove any air pockets. Place a few seeds in the pot and barely cover them with soil.

4 Cover the pot with a clear plastic bag or a piece of plastic wrap and place it in a sunny window. Remove the bag in a few weeks when you see sprouts.

KEEP IT GREEN

• The kiwi plant is a vine, so give it supports to grow on.

OTHER IDEAS

You can grow almonds the same way you grow kiwis. Just plant one seed (nut) per pot. Once your plant is growing well, ask an adult to help you pinch it back to keep it looking thick and bushy.

Papaya

Papayas turn yellow when they're ripe and the seeds are ready to be planted.

GROW IT RIGHT

1 Remove the sac around each seed with your fingers and wipe the seeds with paper towels.

2 Place a layer of stones in the bottom of a pot and mostly fill the pot with potting soil. Gently pack down the soil to remove any air pockets. Place a few seeds in the pot and cover them with about 1 cm (½ in.) of soil.

3 Cover the pot with a clear plastic bag or a piece of plastic wrap and place it in a sunny window. Keep the soil moist and remove the bag in about two weeks when you see sprouts.

KEEP IT GREEN

• Give your papaya plants lots of sun and fertilizer (be sure to follow the directions on the package). Keep them in a humid spot, away from drafts.

• Papaya seedlings are easily infected by fungus, so water them only when the soil begins to feel dry.

CAN YOU BELIEVE IT?

People in Central America have known for hundreds of years that papayas contain a substance called papain that tenderizes meat. Today papain is an important part of meat tenderizers that you buy at the grocery store.

OTHER IDEAS

Pomegranates can be grown in the same way as papayas, but it may take four weeks for these sprouts to show. Be sure to always keep the soil around your pomegranate plant moist, except in the winter when the plant takes a rest.

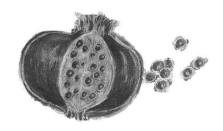

Mango

You can use any kind of ripe mango for planting.

GROW IT RIGHT

1 Remove the seed from the mango and scrub it well. Ask an adult to use a serrated knife to scrape off all the fruit. Let the seed dry overnight.

2 To remove the husk from the seed, ask an adult to make a small nick in the husk where you see a little indentation. Use the knife to gently pull the edges of the husk apart. Make sure you don't damage the seed.

3 Place a layer of stones in the bottom of a pot and mostly fill the pot with potting soil. Gently pack down the soil to remove any air pockets. Place the seed flat in the pot and cover it with about 0.5 cm (¼ in.) of soil.

4 Cover the pot with a clear plastic bag or a piece of plastic wrap and put it in a sunny window. Keep the soil moist and remove the bag in about three weeks when you see sprouts.

KEEP IT GREEN

• Give your mango plant lots of sun. Its leaves are bright red but turn green within a few weeks.

HOE, HOE, HOE

What did one grumpy mango tree say to the other?

"Leaf me alone!"

Fruit salad

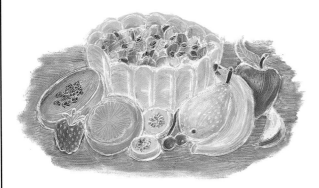

Mango, watermelon, orange, apple, kiwi — mix together the fruits in this section and you've got a great fruit salad. You can also add bananas, berries, pears, peaches, grapes or other fruits.

• Choose different-colored fruits and cut them in a variety of shapes and sizes.

• Pour orange juice over your salad to prevent the fruit from drying out and to help it from turning brown. It's the ascorbic acid in the juice that prevents the darkening. You can use lemon, lime or grapefruit juice too.

• If you like, sweeten your salad by adding a little sugar (white or brown), honey or maple syrup.

• Add crunch to your salad by sprinkling on some nuts or muesli.

• If you're not going to grow the pineapple top (see page 12), cut the fruit and its leaves in half, as shown. Scoop out the fruit and serve your fruit salad in the pineapple bowl. You can also serve your salad in hollowed-out melons, avocados or oranges.

• Fruit salad tastes delicious on its own, or spoon it over yogurt, ice cream, meringue or gingerbread.

Avocado

The best type of avocado for growing is the ripe, large, green-skinned kind.

GROW IT RIGHT

1 Remove the brown skin from the avocado pit by scrubbing it.

2 Ask an adult to help you stick toothpicks around the middle of the pit.

3 Balance the pit on the rim of a glass of water so that the flat end of the pit faces down and the bottom third of the pit is in the water, as shown. Place the glass in a warm place that isn't too sunny.

4 Keep the water at the same level and change it weekly.

5 When the roots from the pit are at least 7.5 cm (3 in.) long, plant the avocado in a small pot so that half of the pit sticks out of the soil. Your avocado plant will grow best in a warm, sunny place.

KEEP IT GREEN

• Make sure the soil is always moist but never soggy.

• Your avocado tree will take a rest during the winter. Let the soil really dry out between waterings — but don't let the plant droop — until you see new leaves growing in the spring.

HOE, HOE, HOE

What's yellow on the inside and green on the outside?

A banana disguised as an avocado!

Guacamole

Dip in with tortilla chips — delicious!
This recipe will provide you with two
avocado pits to grow.

YOU WILL NEED

2	ripe avocados	
250 mL	mayonnaise	1 c.
½	onion, finely chopped	
1	medium tomato, chopped	
	salt and pepper, to taste	
10 mL	lemon juice	2 tsp.
3 or 4 drops	Tabasco sauce	

UTENSILS
small kitchen knife, medium bowl, fork, plastic wrap

1 Peel and pit the avocados with the knife. Place the avocado pulp in the bowl and mash it with the fork.

2 Add the rest of the ingredients to the avocado and mix well. Add more Tabasco sauce if you like your guacamole spicy.

3 Place plastic wrap over the bowl so that it is resting on the surface of the guacamole (this will help to prevent it from turning brown).

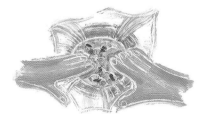

4 Refrigerate the guacamole overnight or until the flavors are blended.

FROM THE GROUND UP

The plants in this section
all grow from tubers or bulbs.
A tuber is part of the stem, but it grows
underground and is covered with bumps
that can grow into buds. It often grows
across or along the soil. A bulb stores
everything the plant needs to make
leaves (and flowers) and sends
leaves up and roots down.

Some of the plants in this section
grow in soil, some grow on stones
and some grow on both. Follow the
instructions for each one to produce
beautiful leaves and flowers — and
even some vegetables to eat.

Garlic

*Garlic grows in buds, which are made up
of many smaller pieces, called cloves.*

GROW IT RIGHT

1 Place a layer of stones in a bowl or
dish with sides.

2 Remove the papery covering from
a few cloves of garlic and stand
them up on the stones so that their
pointy ends face up and the ends where
they attach to the rest of the bulb are on
the stones. If you need to, add a few
more stones to hold each clove so it
stands up straight. (See page 8 for extra
tips on how to grow plants on stones.)

3 Pour in enough water to cover the bottom of the cloves.

KEEP IT GREEN

• Place your garlic cloves in a sunny window so that the shoots will turn a deep green.

• You can eat the shoots your garlic sends up — just snip off the tips and add them to salads or any other dishes that you'd like to give a garlicky taste.

FOR YOUR TABLE

If you plant garlic cloves in soil, they will grow into whole bulbs that you can eat. Prepare a pot with a layer of stones at the bottom (for drainage) and half fill the pot with soil. Stand the cloves on the soil, pointy ends up, and cover them with about 2.5 cm (1 in.) of soil.

Keep the pot in a sunny window and let the soil dry out a little between waterings. Fertilize the plants twice a month. You will have to care for your garlic for a few months, but each clove you plant will grow into a bulb made up of many cloves. You can plant your garlic cloves outside in the same way, if you like.

OTHER IDEAS

Place onions root side down on a dish of stones and grow them the same way as garlic is grown.

Potato

Not only can your potato plants grow to be 1 m (3 ft.) tall with purple flowers, but they'll also give you little potatoes that you can eat.

GROW IT RIGHT

1 Use old potatoes that have buds or sprouts growing out of them. Cut your potatoes into chunks that each have at least one bud.

2 Put the chunks on a sunny windowsill for two days so they dry out and harden a little (this keeps them from rotting underground).

3 Prepare a pot with a layer of stones at the bottom and half fill the pot with soil. Place the chunks in the pot, bud side up, and cover them with about 2.5 cm (1 in.) of soil.

KEEP IT GREEN

• Keep the potatoes in a sunny window and water them when dry.

• If any of the potatoes push up out of the soil, cover them with a little more soil. Otherwise, they'll turn green and poisonous.

CAN YOU BELIEVE IT?

Did you know that potato flakes are sometimes used as snowflakes in films?

Pressing flowers

With a lot of patience and sun, your plants may flower for you. To keep these flowers for a long time, try pressing them. This method works for any flowers you want to dry, but flat flowers that aren't very thick dry best. You can also press leaves. Keep the flowers as a reminder of the plants you've grown, or follow the directions on this page to make gifts and cards.

1 Place freshly picked flowers or leaves between two pieces of paper towel and put this "sandwich" between the pages of a heavy book.

2 Put the book in a warm, dry place and place more heavy books on top of it.

3 After one week, carefully check your flowers or leaves to see if they are dry. If they are damp or stick to the paper towels, place them back between the towels and book pages and leave them for another week.

4 Glue your plants to notepaper and cover them with clear, self-adhesive plastic. You can make bookmarks, gift tags or place cards in the same way.

Ginger

It's those funny-looking knobs and bumps on a piece of ginger that grow into stems and long, green leaves.

GROW IT RIGHT

1 Prepare a pot with a layer of stones at the bottom and mostly fill the pot with soil.

2 Lay the piece of ginger flat in the pot and barely cover it with soil — gardeners say that ginger likes to have its "back" out of the soil.

3 Keep the soil moist and place the pot in a sunny window to keep the ginger warm.

KEEP IT GREEN

• The ginger will send up shoots that grow quickly. Don't worry if some die — new ones will soon replace them.

• Within two months, your ginger shoots may be as tall as 1 m (3 ft.). Don't eat the shoots, but you can cut a small bit off the end of the piece of ginger and use it in recipes.

HOE, HOE, HOE

How do you stop a dog from digging up your garden?

Hide the shovel!

Ginger-almond slices

Buy a large piece of ginger so that after you've chopped enough for these cookies, you'll have a piece to plant.

YOU WILL NEED

125 mL	butter, softened	½ c.
500 mL	brown sugar	2 c.
2	eggs	
5 mL	vanilla	1 tsp.
50 mL	fresh ginger, finely chopped	¼ c.
750 mL	all-purpose flour	3 c.
5 mL	baking soda	1 tsp.
175 mL	toasted almonds, chopped	¾ c.

UTENSILS
large bowl, wooden spoon, waxed paper, small, sharp knife, baking sheets lined with aluminum foil

1 In the large bowl, beat together the butter and brown sugar. Beat in the eggs and vanilla until creamy. Stir in the ginger.

2 Add the flour, baking soda and nuts and stir.

3 Shape the dough into a log about 5 cm (2 in.) wide and 35 cm (14 in.) long. Wrap the dough in waxed paper and refrigerate for at least 4 hours.

4 Preheat the oven to 200°C (400°F). Ask an adult to help you cut the log into slices 0.5 cm (¼ in.) thick. Place the slices 1 cm (½ in.) apart on the baking sheets. Ask an adult to help you bake the slices for about 10 to 12 minutes or until golden. Place the cookies on a rack to cool. Makes about 60 cookies.

Decorating pots

You can decorate plastic or clay pots. First make sure your pots are clean and dry. Then try these ideas to make your pots look unique. (See page 13 to find out how to prepare clay pots for decorating.)

• Cover a pot with découpage. Mix equal amounts of white glue and water, dip strips of colored paper in the mixture, and smooth them onto your pot. When the découpage is dry, cover it with two coats of acrylic varnish.

• Glue on beads, buttons, shells or pressed flowers (see page 37).

• Wrap on colored string. Paint the string, cover the pot with glue, and wind the string around the pot. Or use the string to make a design on the pot.

• Make an antique-looking pot with masking tape and brown liquid shoe polish. Cover your pot with scraps of masking tape. Shake the polish well, then dab on a coat. Let it dry, then add more coats until you get the color you like. Be sure the pot dries well between coats. When the pot is completely dry, add two coats of acrylic varnish.

OTHER CONTAINERS

You can use many containers besides flowerpots for growing your plants: cans, glasses, plastic containers, mugs, teacups and saucers, etc. Place a saucer or other waterproof dish under your container to protect the surface it's on from soil and water.